AUM

The Eternal Energy

AUM

The Eternal energy

Techniques for Stability, Strength, Stress Management and Healing

Dr. Vinod Verma

Gayatri Books International

Declaimer: The book is written for the purpose of education and for leading a spiritual life. The parts on healing are not meant to replace the services of a physician. The author and the publisher are in no way responsible for any medical claims regarding the material presented in this book. For using methods provided in this book at commercial level requires the prior permission from the author. For more information, write to the author directly.

Copyright © Dr. Vinod Verma. First published in German and English in 2007 under the title, AUM as Infinite Energy.
Present revised edition, copyright © Dr. Vinod Verma 2014

All right reserved. No part of this book may be reproduced or transmitted in any form or by any means, mechanical or electronic including recording, photocopying or any information storage and retrieval system without the written permission from the author. Brief passages may be quoted by the reviewers and commentators.

Published by Gayatri Books International, Himalayan Centre, Village Astal, Dunda, Uttarkashi-249151 (Uttarkhanda), India. Any legal matters will be handled in the jurisdiction of this address.

Translation rights are held by the author. Write to her directly at ayurvedavv@yahoo.com or ayurvedavv@gmail.com.

Visit Dr. Vinod Verma at www.ayurvedavv.com and www.drvinodverma.com to find out about her other publications and activities like seminars, lectures, consultations, etc. Look for more information on the last pages of the book.

Consultant: Mohit Joshi

Cover design and photographs by the author

ISBN: 978-81-89514-26-6

Foreword

"Aumityaitadakṣaramidam sarvam
tasyaupavyākhyānam
bhūtam bhavad bhavishyaditi
Sarvamaunkāra aiva yacchānyat
trikālāteetam
tadaspyaunkara aiva"

"AUM is an imperishable word. AUM is universe and this is the exposition of AUM. The present, the past and the future, all that was, all that is, and all that will be is AUM. Likewise, all else that may exist beyond the bound of time, that too is AUM."
(*Mandukya Upanishad* I, 1)

The supreme word-principle (*Śabda-brahman*) is described in the Vedas under various names. It identified with mind, matter and *prajapati*. In the Rig Veda it is conceived as the 'active power of Brahman', it is identified with It and is personified as a 'productive principle'. *Vāk*– the speech is held together by AUM just as leaves are held together by one leaf stalk and AUM is the entire world. The true significance of the

AUM: The Eternal Energy

Vedas is contained in the syllable AUM that has also been equated with *Pranava* (lit. that which resound) and *udgitha* (lit. upward song). Its repetition as bee*ja* mantra (seed, from which all other mantras have been born) ensures retention of knowledge gained, protection of the seeker against error and misfortune, and to enhance concentration of the mind which can lead to bliss. The sage *Patanjali*, foremost exponent of the Yoga speaks of the Supreme Eternal as an actual cosmic sound of AUM heard in meditation.

For the purpose of *Sadhanā* (spiritual practice) the seeker is asked to imagine four parts in Brahman, or Cosmic Energy. They are called four quarters. The first three – gross, subtle, and causal- constitute the phenomenal world. The fourth is transcendental, being beyond time, space and causality. It is Turiya or the unconditioned Brahman, Brahman and Atman are identical. The gross aspect of Brahman has its counterpart in the working state (*visva*) of Atman, when the external world is perceived by means of the sense-organs. The subtle aspect, in the dream state (*Taijasa*) is when the internal world, created by working experiences, is perceived; and the causal aspect is experienced in deep sleep (*Prājna*), characterized by bliss and cessation of mental activity. The transcendental aspect of Atman, or Pure Consciousness, which is Its true nature, is the same as *Turiya*. Like Brahman AUM also has four parts, called letters (mātra). The first three are A, U, and M, corresponding to the first three quarters of Brahman and Atman. In addition to these three is an undifferentiated sound of AUM, which comes after the first three letters are pronounced. Devoid of all characteristics, it is not any particular sound, but it denotes the subtraction of all sounds. It is the same as the unconditioned Brahman, or *Turiya*. Thus through meditation with AUM, one can realize Brahman in its worldly and in its cosmic aspects.

The sound A– the first letter of AUM pervades all sound. It is present in all sounds. No sound can be produced without opening the mouth, and the sound that is thus produced is A. Likewise, the entire universe is pervaded by *vaisvanara* Atman. The knowledge of the dream state and of deep sleep is possible only in waking state. Since the three states constitute our entire experience of the universe, the waking state pervades the whole universe. Although A, being the first of all letters, is superior to them all, U that comes after A is also superior in a figurative sense. *Taijasa* or Atman functioning through the dream state is again said to be superior to *vaisvānara* because it perceives ideas, whereas the latter sees only gross object. While investigating dreams the seekers realizes physical phenomena to be states of the mind, and that knowledge brings him nearer to the truth. As the letter U is between A and M, so the dream state is between waking and deep sleep. *Prajna Ātman*, whose sphere is deep sleep, is M, the third letter of AUM. Both the waking state and the dream state during manifestation emerge from and during non-manifestation disappear into the dreamless state. Therefore, both *Vaisvanara* and *Taijas* are said to be contained in *Prājna* which may be compared to the container. When the word AUM is repeated quickly several times, the sound actually heard is *manm*. That is why the letter A and U become one with M. Likewise, *Visva* and *Taijasa* become one with, or merge in, *Prajnā* in deep sleep.

The phenomenal world consists of ideas or mental states. Ideas depend upon words for their expression. The utterance of the word AUM (A...U...M.) gives the clue to the pronunciation of all words or sounds uttered by human beings. The various parts of the vocal organ that are used in utterance of all sounds are also used in the pronunciation of AUM. Therefore, AUM is the matrix of all sounds, which in their diversified forms give rise to the words used in language. The sound A, coming from the throat when the mouth opens to utter any word is the beginning of all sounds. The sound M is the final sound when the lips are closed. And the sound U is the rolling forward of the impulse which has been created in the throat and which ends with the closing of the lips. Thus, when AUM is uttered, all the diverse parts of the vocal organ needed for uttering words are used. Therefore, AUM includes all sounds. The substratum of all sounds is AUM and the substratum of phenomena is Brahman. The sound signifying the phenomena is non-different from the phenomena, since both are illusory. When the illusion disappears, there remains only the substratum, which is one and is without any differentiation. Therefore, it is said that Brahman is AUM.

With reference to Atman, *Visva* merges in *Taijasa*, and *Taijasa* in Prajna, similarly, with reference to AUM, the sound A merges in U, and U in M. the different aspects of Atman are identical with the different sounds of AUM. He who knows this identity also realizes that the entire universe of waking and dreaming merges in *Prajna* and emerges from it. This *prajna* is *Isvara*, or Brahman regarded as the cause of the universe. Through meditation on A, the seeker attains *Visva*; through meditation on U, *Taijasa*; and through meditation on M, *Prajna*. Meditation on the "Soundless" brings no attainment. The positive result of the knowledge of Turiya is cessation of duality that produces friction, fear and suffering. By meditating on AUM in the heart as a symbol of Brahman the aspirant becomes free from all kinds of fear and friction and enjoys the bliss of the highest heaven.

The present book entitled "AUM: The infinite energy" is a unique contribution of Dr. Vinod Verma to mankind. The book is not merely an analysis of conceptual speculation but the profound product of spiritual practice she has constantly been performing for several decades. As a spiritual teacher she teaches some simple and easy techniques to reach the profound part of our consciousness, attain mental stability and evoke the energy present within. By practicing these techniques with mantra AUM one can use one's own immense energy for getting mental-physical strength and equilibrium, the very basis of peace and blissfulness.

Dharmanand Sharma
Philosophy Department
Panjab University, Chandigarh

Mountain AUM in the high Himalayas

Preface

The purpose of this little book is to evoke the subtle energy within us, which we have in abundance and are unable to use. We have this energy in dormant form and it is the cause of our being. It is important to recognise the cause of consciousness in our bodies and learn to awaken the subtle energy by using various techniques.

I have given simple techniques in this book for attaining inner stillness (sattva) with which you can get rid of the tension, stress, irritants and troubles of everyday life. You have troubles because you recognise only the troubles and give them importance. The moment you realise their transitory nature and the eternal nature of the cause of being, you will see your troubles like a sand grain in camel's mouth.

With gradual practice of the techniques provided in this book, you will reach a higher state of mind (*buddhi*). You will develop lucidity and intuition and your work efficiency will enhance many folds. The advantage of these techniques is that they are simply imbibed in your daily routine and you do not need any extra time, sitting sessions or doing malas (rosary) with a mantra. They bring your mind to sattva (the inner stillness and peace) and you reach a yogic state while being totally in the world. This is a path of a karmayogi and in the Bhagavad Gita, Shree Krishna has explained it in one shloka:

"Brahmaarpanam Brahma havirbrahmaagnau brahmnaa hutam,
Brahmaiv ten gantavyam Brahmakarma smaadhinaa"[*]

A yogi is performing a Yajna, he offers ghee mixed with other herbs to the holy fire with a ladle and it is supposed to get to Brahma (the Eternal Energy). The essence of this shloka is that the person who is performing is Brahman, the ladle with which he is offering is Brahman, the offering he is putting in the fire is Brahman, the fire itself is Brahman and this offering is aimed to reach Brahman.[**]

---

[*] Bhagavad Gita, IV, 24
[**] The word Brahman in Sanatana dharma is used for the Eternal Cosmic Energy or the Universal Soul.

Preface

There is a constant transformation of energy from one form into the other. Our normal day-to-day situations are not that of a yogi, but to balance this transformation of energy is equally essential for us. By balancing this energy, we can solve many of our nagging problems which make our lives unpleasant, give us mental tension and ultimately make us sick. This balance can be attained effortlessly by doing some simple practices provided in this book.
The principal purpose of the book is to imbibe spirituality in our daily lives for balancing the mind and for using our own immense energy for getting

mental and physical strength, equilibrium, intuitive power, enhancing work efficiency and learning ability to heal.

Vinod Verma   December 2006
www.ayurvedavv.com
www.drvinodverma.com
ayurvedavv@yahoo.com
                                  Present edition 2014

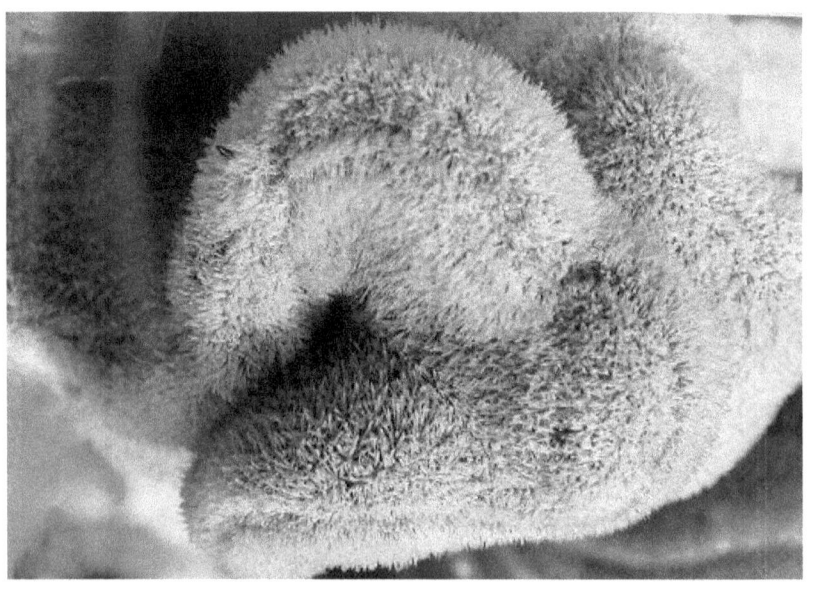

Symbol of AUM on an animal in the high Himalayas

Contents

Foreword	5
Preface	11
Acknowledgements	17
Introduction	19

Part I
Aum: The Eternal Cosmic Energy — 27

Part II
Body: The temple of Eternal Energy — 35

Part III
Consciousness of the Eternal Energy — 47

Part IV
Evoking the Eternal Energy (Physical) — 57

Part V
Evoking the Eternal Energy (Subtle) — 67

Part VI
Benefits of the Eternal Energy — 73

AUM: The Eternal Energy

Part VII

Healing the Mind with AUM   81

Part VIII

Healing the Body with AUM   89

AUM: Your Inner Guru and Protector   101

   About the Author   *111*

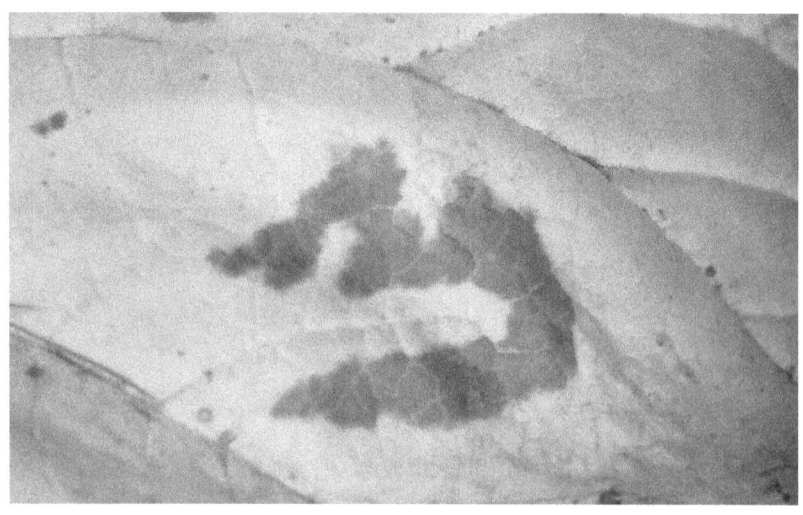

AUM on a winter leaf in the high Himalayas

Acknowledgements

I am indebted to Professor Dharmananda Sharma of Panjab University for guiding me with his immense source of wisdom and also writing foreword for the book. He is always generous with his time and knowledge.

I express my gratitude to Mahendra Kulasrestha for his editorial work. I express my warm thanks to Mohit Joshi for his divine patience to help me with the computer odds and for donating one computer for our Himalayan Centre where we had lost our office in a fire.

I thank my nephew Pranav for helping me with the AUM illustrations.

My special thanks go to Swami Sundranand ji of Gangotri for providing me the exceptional pictures of the symbol AUM in the high Himalayas (see page 10, 14, 16 and 18). He is a unique yogi with a camera who has a distinctive endowment of photographing the high Himalayas also in winter. He has published a book with his exclusive collection of photographs, *Himalayas through the Lens of a Sadhu*.

I am grateful to Lokandra Bisht of Uttarkashi for putting me in touch with Swami Sundranand ji and making his pictures available for this book.

AUM: The Eternal Energy

Symbol of AUM in the clouds of high Himalayas

Introduction

The origin of the mantra AUM (mostly written as OM) is from the Vedic tradition. The Vedas do not propound any religion. They are the source of universal wisdom that explains the cosmic order called the *Sanatana Dharma*. 'Sanatana' means eternal and 'Dharma' means cosmic order. The cosmic order is never ending and it is eternal. That is why it is represented by a chakra or wheel called Dharma Chakra.

Chakra representing the Eternal notion of time from Konark Sun temple in Orrisa

AUM: The Eternal Energy

Before proceeding further, it is important to understand that the word 'Hindu' which is also associated with the so-called Hindu religion, is basically a linguistic error. During the Vedic times, there was Indus civilization along the Sindhu and Sarasvati rivers on the Indian continent. The neighbouring Persians had difficulty in pronouncing 'S' and they pronounced the river as 'Hindu' instead. This was communicated to the rest of the world and the people of the subcontinent became known as Hindus in the world, further giving rise to the words like Industan, Hindustan, and so on. Whatever we may call them, the people of the subcontinent gave to the world tremendous wisdom. Vedas and Upanishads, Yoga, Ayurveda, Bhagavad Gita, astronomy, physics, astrology, etc. are the heritage of humanity from this subcontinent. The cyclic notion of time, theories on cosmogony and cosmology and the notion of the holistic are some of the other concepts from India which are valued in the modern world. After a disintegrated way of living and thinking, the western world is returning to the notion of holistic which implies that the same principles govern the whole cosmos, whether it is a tree, human body or the astronomical system.

Unfortunately by the colonisers of India, the Sanatana dharma was presented as 'Hinduism' to the rest of the world. The western world looked at our tradition with a narrow vision. It should be understood that the different doctrines were developed on the Indian continent for a common goal and they are all a part of the Sanatana dharma which denotes the order governing the cosmos in all its manifestation: cosmic, spiritual, social, cultural, scientific, and so on. The Sanatana dharma has no founder and it denotes the eternal norms or the universal principles. It has no beginning and no end. The basic goal of the dharma is the maintenance of harmony in the cosmos. Human beings are a part of the cosmos like the rest. There is a constant change and everything is inter-related, interdependent and inter-connected. There is nothing without a definite function and there is exact selection of means for the production of a definite end. There is never a random combination of events and there is order, regulation, system and division of functions.

Sanatana dharma flourished along the Sindhu and Sarasvati rivers in the West and along the Ganga and Yamuna rivers in the east of Northern part of the Indian continent. All these rivers and other historical sites of this ancient civilisation are mentioned in the Vedas. It is important to know for the reader that the symbol of AUM is found in the seals of the ancient Sindhu civilisation which flourished before 3000 B.C. Following are two

AUM: The Eternal Energy

illustrations from these seals. There is the Mahayoga and the symbol AUM. The writing on the Mahayogi seal is from the pre-Sanskrit era.

AUM represents the fundamental message of the Sanatana dharma in the shortest form, in both tone and image. It represents the cosmic reality, which is the combination of the matter and energy. In human beings, these are in the form of body and soul. The destructible body is the temple of the indestructible and eternal soul. With the repetition of AUM, we are able to withdraw the senses and silence the mind. Once the mind is silenced, we are able to reach the Eternal Energy of the soul. After having access to this immense source of energy, we can use it for various beneficial purposes.

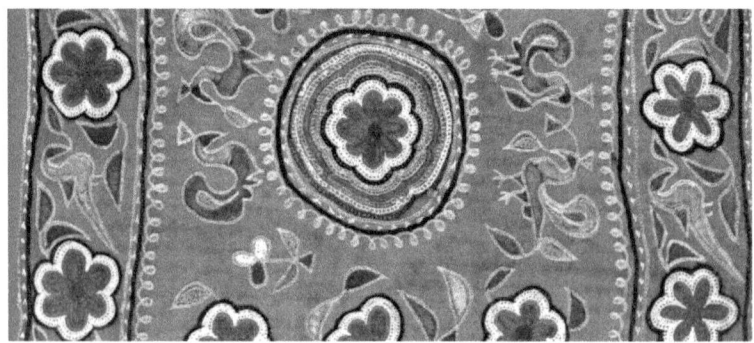

Introduction

Mahayogi (above) and figure AUM (below) from the seals of
Mohenjadaro (The Indus Valley civilization), 3000 B.C.

The book offers practical methods to harness the energy, which lies untapped within us. We do not need any special sessions or lessons for this purpose; it is a matter of personal effort and persistence. The results are beautiful– we can attain peace, harmony, radiance and health. By following the simple methods given in this book, you can purify yourself mentally and physically.

A Vedic Payer

I translate below a Vedic Prayer in Hindi sung after the completion of a Yajana in North West India. This prayer is 150 years old and shows the emphasis of the Vedas on the fundamental human values and on the entire cosmic environment.

Oh mighty One! Purify our minds,
Give us the mental strength to get rid of falsification and dubious ways!

May we recite the Vedic hymns and remain truthful,
May all of us be constantly happy and go beyond the ocean of grief!

May we perform yajana for the well being
of humanity,
May we benefit the humanity by remaining
on the path of dharma and follow its guiding
principles!

May we perform yajana each day with
reverence and devotion,
May we alleviate the suffering humanity
from pain and disease!

May our minds be free from the evil and
criminal attributes,
May the Yjana bless men and women for the
fulfilment of their desires!

May this havana (the fire ceremony) be
beneficial to each living being,
May there be good air and water with
fragrance everywhere!

May we get rid of our selfish intentions and
the love amongst us enhances,
May each one of us behave selflessly and be
humble!

We pray with joint hands and bend our heads with respect,
Oh mighty one, the incarnation of compassion, shower your compassion upon us!

Part I
AUM: The Eternal Cosmic Energy

1. The sound and symbol of AU……..M… represents the cosmic reality.

The first part of the sound begins with a long AU…… This is a sound like 'o' in oval in English, like 'au' is pronounced in French and like 'o' in ohne in German. The second part of the sound ends with a nasal 'm' which is also a prolonged sound.

The mantra AUM is the smallest mantra and it comes to us from the Vedic tradition of the Sanatana dharma. The Vedic language is the only language in the world which is sound and tonality dominant. In fact, in the Indian tradition until recent times, everything was written in poetry and a writer is called poet. The process of learning is also with singing. In the traditional schools, even grammar and mathematics are taught by singing. AUM is considered as an eternal sound, which is complete by itself and is the source of all other sounds. That is why, AUM is called the seed of all the other mantras (beej mantra) and is used in the beginning of the other mantras.

> **2. The first part of the symbol AUM, which is represented by something like the shape of three (3), signifies the diversity of the cosmos.**

The cosmos has diverse forms, colours and creatures. Everywhere, there is action taking place— there are mountains, forests, lakes, rivers, seas and oceans. There are varieties of plants and animals which beautify this cosmos. There are days, nights, seasons and everything is constantly changing. No two human beings look alike and leaves of each species of plants differ. Diversity, change and beauty are the characteristics of our cosmos and the first part of AUM represents these in both form and sound.

> **3. Gradually the sound remounts.**

With the gradual practice, you will enhance the capacity of your lungs to take a deeper breath and to prolong the time of the sound of AU…. As you

Aum: The Eternal Cosmic Energy

chant this, the sound should remount. However, in the initial stages, you may not be able to do that for long. One requires a repeated practice of pranayama (breathing exercises) for mounting and prolonging the sound.

4. **The sound of AU... is then changed to nasal M... during the last part of the breath and it rises to the head region.**

The second part of AUM is the nasal M..... with the sound rising in the head and is symbolised by half-moon and a point on it. At the peak of AU......, the lips are closed and the sound of nasal m..... comes out from the nose. You will feel this sound raising and resounding in your head region. By this time, you are mostly out of breath. Thus, prolongation of breathing is essential to be able to sing this part in harmony with the previous part.

Learning to Pronounce AUM

1. Sit down cross-legged or in another comfortable posture, straighten your back and take a deep breath. Hold the breath for a brief moment and begin to release it gradually. Make sure that the outflow of the

breath is smooth and it is not in a stop-and-go manner. Repeat this for at least five breaths.

2. This step is the same as above, but this time, release your breath with a sound from the deeper part of your throat. This is not yet the sound of AU... we are aiming at. Make sure that your mouth is closed while you do this breathing exercise. Repeat this also for at least five times.

3. Take a deep breath and slowly release it while making the sound of AU...... from the upper part of your throat. In this process, your lips will slightly open and curl. Repeat this also five times.

4. For singing the complete AUM, do the step three and at the end of AU...., gradually transform this tone into a nasal M. The sound of M... should mount towards your head region.

5. **The diversity of the cosmos fuses into oneness during the pronunciation of AU……..M…….**

The transformation of the first melody into the second of AUM signifies a journey from the phenomenal world of form, colour, action (karma), movement and change to the still, eternal and unchangeable energy. This energy is the cause of action in the phenomenal world but is Itself away from all actions. By Itself, it cannot act, as it is mere energy without matter, which is the vehicle for action. The matter can act, only after this energy brings life to it.

6. **AUM symbolises the Cosmic Energy (Universal Soul) and the Cosmic Substance (matter).**

Explaining further the previous sutra, here is the clarification of two distinct energies which are the cause of the phenomenal world when they submerge into each other. Cosmic Energy is the Eternal Energy, whereas Cosmic Substance is the material energy. Without the Cosmic Energy, the material energy does not react. The phenomenal world comes to being only by the fusion of these two principal energies. Thus, AUM symbolises both these energies which are the cause of our existence.

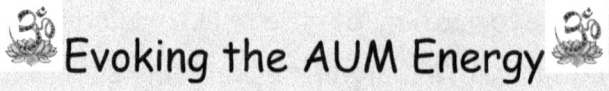 Evoking the AUM Energy

Concentrate on the figurative form of AUM. Always keep this image in your mind. For doing this, put it on different places where you can see it often.

Listen to its music. The suggested music CD is from Pandit Jasraj, a singer of Indian classical music. Although there are numerous CDs available, but this one is sung in a meditative state by this great musician.

By doing so, you are seeing and listening to the symbol that signifies the fascinating diversity of the universe and that diversity dissolving into oneness that binds us all with each other and with the rest of the cosmos. You do not need extra time and effort for doing the above-said practice. Nevertheless, you will see the positive results. You will attain inner quietness and peace.

After doing the above practices and the previously described practice of breathing and singing AUM, this mother of all sounds will become a source of energy and peace for you.

7. **The repetition of the mantra AUM is called pranava.**

The repetition of the mantra AUM is called pranava in the Vedic tradition. In other words, pranava is the technical term used for the repetition of the mantra AUM. This term is also used by Patanjali in the Yogasutra (see Part III, sutra 9 for more details).

AUM: The Eternal Energy

Part II
Body. The Temple of Eternal Energy

1. The two principal cosmic energies the syllable AUM symbolises are also present in the human body.

Same principles of cosmic reality apply to the universe as to the human body or other living systems. The Eternal Energy is everywhere in the cosmos and so is the Cosmic Substance, as the phenomenal world is the result of the combination of these two, and they are both merged into each other.

Before we learn to evoke the Eternal Energy present within us in subtle form, it is important to understand the fundamentals of our bodily existence in this cosmos.

2. **The body has two separate entities merged into each other– the visible and the invisible.**

The visible entity is our physical reality, whereas the invisible entity is that energy which puts life into the visible. It is easy to understand this concept by taking an example of the transformation from life to death. When an alive person dies, he/she has the same body bulk and form of the brain is intact in the skull, but nevertheless, this person is not able to move or think, as the invisible entity that made the visible entity function is no more there. It is 'flown out' of the body, therefore causing what we call death. After the invisible entity has left the body, the body does not remain as an independent system any more. It decays because it does not have any of its subsystems like the immune system, nervous system, respiratory system, and so on.

3. **The visible entity (body) is destructible but has transformable energy which has its continuum.**

In the previous sutra, it is said that the body destroys when the Eternal Energy is separated from it. However, it does not mean that the visible entity of a human being goes to nothingness. The body as a system is no more there, but the bigger system (the cosmic system) goes on with its functions. The visible entity is transformed and goes back to its cosmic material. It is from the same cosmic material that the new bodies are made for those who are conceived and born to exist as independent entities. Individuals have their karmic continuity in terms of their destructible entity or physical being. From the karma of the previous life, the circumstances and conditions of the next birth are decided. Besides that, the fundamental character of an individual, external appearance, his/her basic attitudes and aptitudes are decided by the result of the past karma.

4. The body is made of the five fundamental elements.

All what exists is made of five elements, which form the basic structure of all the visible entities in the cosmos. The first element is space, as without it nothing can exist. In space exists air, which is the living force for all beings. The third element is fire and the previous two elements are essential for its existence. The fourth element is water and its existence is dependent on the previous three elements. For example without heat, the water freezes and cannot flow. The fifth element is earth, which contains all the previous four elements as well.

Kedarnath temple (Shiva) in the high Himalayas

5. **The invisible, indestructible and Eternal Energy can be only alive if it inhabits the transformable energy.**

What we call 'alive' or to be living is only possible when the visible and invisible entities come together as one. The invisible Eternal Energy by itself is not alive until it inhabits the visible material body made of five elements.

6. **Body is the temple of soul, which is a part of the Cosmic Energy or the Universal Soul.**

Soul is divinity in the body. Divine is that which is eternal and not destructible, as compared to human body and other living beings in the universe which come to an end after a certain lifespan. According to the Vedic tradition, Brahman or the Universal Soul is present in each one of us and as has been explained above, it makes the material body alive.
The relationship of the visible and invisible entities is described as the temple and the divinity in this sutra.

7. **To keep this temple clean and pure is the foremost dharma of all human beings.**

Our first duty (svadharma) is towards our body. An individual should keep the body clean and in rhythm with the rest of the cosmos, as it is the abode of the Eternal Energy. This energy radiates in each cell of the body and keeps it alive. When we do not maintain our body well, the radiations are blocked and we get out of the cosmic rhythm and suffer from ailments.

It is equally important to keep the mind pure and stable, and human beings should exercise restraint. The yogic tradition is based on this theme of mind control in order to reach the divinity present within us and then to merge this individual soul into the cosmic Eternal Energy.

Amarnath (Shiva Linga) cave temple in Kashmir

8. Body has both dosha and guna.

The body according to the Vedic tradition is all that substance that destroys upon death. Thus, the capability of thinking is a part of the body. Mind is considered as the sixth sense, which is superior to all senses, as it controls the other five senses.

Body: The Temple of Eternal Energy

Like everything in the cosmos, body is made of five elements: ether, air, fire, water and earth. Any living being from plant or animal kingdom has an independent system which functions on the same principles as the cosmic system. The five elements take the form of the three vital forces to perform all the physical and mental functions of the body. These vital forces are called dosha. These are– vata (constituted of ether and air), pitta (constituted of fire) and kapha (constituted of water and earth).

The living body has an independent thinking capability, which has three characteristic qualities or guna. These are sattva (comprises of qualities like stillness, peace, goodness, beauty, and so on), rajas (comprises of characteristics of movements, impetus, action, and so on) and tamas (all those qualities which hinder motion and action, as well as development of mind).

These are the six dimensions of a being. But these six are functional only in the presence of the seventh dimension— the soul. Thus, the totality of our being has seven dimensions.

9. Soul is nirguna.

The three characteristic qualities (guna) of the mind described above are the qualities of the Cosmic Substance at the cosmic level. Contrary to that, the Universal Soul is without any characteristic qualities or guna (nirguna). It is just energy, which has neither a form or a substance, nor any characteristic qualities. Our soul is a part of the Universal Soul and thus, is simply energy that puts life into the substance, which is our body.

10. Soul is the cause of being for the body and is its energy system.

It has been already stated in the explanation of the two previous sutras that the soul puts life into the body and thus is the cause of being. It is this life-giving force, which forms the energy system of the body.

11. Besides the visible energy flow, there are subtle energy channels in the body that carry the Eternal Energy to diverse parts of the body.

Visible energy flow is breathing, blood circulation, digestion, excretion and so on. There is also the subtle energy flow. The energy of the soul flows in each cell of the body. This system of the flow of the invisible energy within the body is like an energy body within the physical body. This is called the subtle body or sukshma sharira.

12. Cleaning and purification help enhance the subtle energy flow in the body and give rise to lucidity of mind.

Any kind of dirt in the physical body and any impurity in the thinking process block the flow of subtle energy in the body. Therefore, cleanliness and mental purity is essential in this temple of soul. Purity of the body and the mind leads to mental lucidity and efficiency due to the smooth flow of subtle energy radiating from the soul.

13. Enhancing sattva with personal efforts enlightens one with the Eternal Energy of the soul.

Sattva is the characteristic quality of mind that has goodness, peace and harmony. One must make an effort to enhance sattva quality of mind. Sattva balances both rajas and tamas. When one makes a repeated effort to attain a sattvic mental state and reaches a level of perfect stillness, the mind is directed towards the Eternal Energy of the soul. Mind is between the five senses and soul. Mostly the mind is drawn to the fascinating world of form, colour and sound through five senses. Through sattva, mind obtains stillness, withdraws temporarily from the senses and the world and is directed to the energy of the soul.

14. At the time of death, the soul separates from the body and the prana ceases.

The existence of the body is between birth and death. The body and soul are linked with each other through prana or the inhaling and exhaling. The moment soul imparts from the body, the cosmic connection of the body through prana also ceases.

15. The five constituent elements go back to their main pool.

The body, without soul disintegrates and the five elements that constitute it go back to their cosmic pool.

Body: The Temple of Eternal Energy

16. The indestructible soul however does not join the Cosmic Energy or the Universal Soul, as it is bound to the karma of that particular individual.

The soul of an individual does not go back to the universal soul unlike the five elements of the body to their main pool. The soul of a particular individual is bound to his/her karma. Soul is pure energy but is bound to karma. The results of the karma are saved on it or exist in the form of a code on it. These decide for the circumstances of the birth of an individual in the next life. The individual attains another body in order to sort out the give and take of many of his/her deeds.

17. It acquires another body made of five elements.

The soul loaded with sum total of the karma of an individual drags him/her through another life. Like this, the cycle of life and death goes on.

18. Chanting of mantra AUM and the concentration upon its significance enhances mental lucidity and thus an

awareness to perform right actions (karma).

According to the Sanatana dharma of the Vedic tradition, an individual is responsible for his/her good or bad action. He/she decides to do karma with the sense of discretion or buddhi. Repetition of mantra AUM and concentration upon its significance give rise to mental lucidity and thus good sense to choose right karma for oneself.

Part III
Consciousness of the Eternal Energy

1. **Awareness of the cause of consciousness as a different entity than the physical being is essential.**

It is difficult to be conscious of the cause of consciousness, as the physical entity made of panchabhuta (the five elements that constitute the body) and the energy that blows life into it are completely integrated into each other. To recognise the pure energy, we have to transcend the physical self. This energy is there in each one of us, although outwardly we see a variation in the aura or radiation emitted by people. It is due to the cover of darkness we form around this energy due to our deeds or karma. To understand this concept, imagine a day with dark thick clouds. We do not see the sun and we do not get even enough light. It is a dark day. As all of us are aware, there is merely a cover between the sun and us. We experience this when we take a flight on such a dark and cloudy day. After attaining certain height, we find the bright sunshine. Similarly, our extreme occupation with the world makes a dark cloud around the Eternal Energy, which is within us. Excess of rajas (activities) and tamas (inertia, attachment, competition, jealousy etc.) in our lives and a lack of sattva to balance these two former modifications of the mind enhance the cover of darkness. A sattvic mind reduces this darkness. To enhance sattva, we need to silence our mind, develop qualities like goodness, compassion, selfless service to humanity, kindness and detachment.

2. **The two different energies, which make our existential reality, are not superior or inferior to each other.**

We have already discussed that soul puts life into the body made of five elements and the existence of the living body is not possible either without the soul or without the material body. Although soul is the cause of consciousness, nevertheless, it cannot act or exist alone as a living being. Thus, the visible

Consciousness of the Eternal Energy

and the invisible entities described in Part II are not superior or inferior to each other, but are simply the two indispensable entities for existence. This is essential to understand for attaining the spiritual consciousness. Imagine a beautiful looking temple. You admire its sculpted walls and its architecture. Gradually you go inside the temple. You have to cross several gates of verandas and rooms to reach the *garbhagriha* or *sanctum sanctorum*. Once you reach there, you get the feeling of devotion and attain stillness. You feel the purity of the atmosphere and also observe the other devotees there with the same sentiments. If you analyse your journey from outer to inner, the beautiful temple already makes the atmosphere for devotion and you reach the inner most part of the temple in the end. Both are important for sanctity. Similarly, to excess the energy of the soul, you have to traverse the body. Eternal Energy of the soul is our being and equally important is the material body that the Eternal Energy inhabits for a human identity. Body in the form you have acquired in this life is not eternal, but the deeds or karma done by you in this identity are passed on to you in the form of sanskara and they are expressed in another body in the next life. Since all the bodies are from the same five fundamental elements, and they also express a part of our being from the past through sanskara, they are also not destructible in the real sense of the term.

3. To get awareness of the Eternal Energy, it is needed to silence one's mind.

We are occupied with our body because it is material and sensuous. Energy of the soul is beyond sensuous perception and that is why with a state of mind which is occupied with the world through sensuous perception, it is not possible to get the consciousness about the Eternal Energy. However, when we silence our mind through personal efforts and withdraw the senses, we are automatically connected to the Eternal Energy of the soul. Mind cannot be occupied with two things at a time. Therefore, it is essential to silence the mind from the sensuous and the worldly to get the *darshana* (to be face to face) with the *sanctum sanctorum* of our being.

4. Repetition of mantra AUM can help us to withdraw from rajas and tamas and bring us to the sattva state of mind.

In our day-to-day existence, we are occupied with diverse activities related to our survival. We earn money, we build houses, shop, cook and eat and are busy in hundreds of activities alike. These keep us mentally occupied and this state of active mind is rajas. Activities lead to fatigue and inertness and we come to a tamas state of mind. However, it is possible to perform our daily actions with a sattvic state of mind by repeating mantra AUM and integrating it in our daily thinking process. The practical aspects of this sutra will be more clear in the next two Parts of the book.

> 5. **Controller of the five senses, the mind is generally considered as the sixth and the most superior sense.**

Mind is considered as sixth sense in the Vedic tradition but is superior to the other senses as it controls and coordinates the activities of all the five senses. Thus, according to this tradition, the duality of body and mind is not thinkable.

> 6. **The mind occupies a place between the soul and the senses.**

This sutra explains the previous sutra and clarifies the status of mind in Sanatana dharma of the Vedic tradition. Mind is between the soul and the senses. It can be occupied with either of them, but not with both of them at a time. What happens normally is that it is occupied with the senses, as through them it is connected to the phenomenal world. Senses constantly provide new information to the mind. In state of sleep, senses are partially closed and the previously acquired knowledge is churned in the mind. To get the experience of Eternal Energy of the soul, tremendous personal effort is required to withdraw the mind from the senses and the sensuous world. Once the mind is silenced, it experiences the endless energy of the soul.

7. **When it is not experiencing the sensuous, it is automatically with the Eternal Energy.**

Once the mind is silenced, it acquires identity with the soul and the adept experiences the cause of consciousness– the soul. It is an experience of one's innermost self or the energy that makes the outer self (physical body) function.

8. Oneness of the mind with the Eternal Energy provides abundance of strength and liberation from troubles.

When the mind achieves oneness with the Eternal Energy of the soul, it automatically acquires lucidity and strength. It feels liberated from the pains and troubles of the sensuous world. This is a higher state of consciousness and is above the reality of the phenomenal world, which is reachable through senses.

9. Repetition of the mantra AUM and concentration on its form help us to withdraw from the senses temporarily and have oneness of the mind with the soul.

The last sutra of this part emphasizes on the technique that can be used to withdraw from the sensuous world. The repetition of the mantra AUM and concentration on its figurative form help withdraw from the senses and makes one experience the abundance, eternal and indestructible energy of the soul.

Given below in the box is the explanation of AUM from Patanjali's Yoga Sutra.

Patanjali's explanation of the AUM mantra

The great Guru of the Yoga Sutra has written about the eternal cosmic energy in Part I of his book. Amongst many methods of achieving meditation, one is by repeating and concentrating on mantra AUM. Here is the text of his Sutras 23, 24, 26 to 29 that describe the Eternal Energy.

" A profound devotion to Ishvara also helps attain meditation. Ishvara is defined as that which is untouched by afflictions, karma and their fruits and the consequent desires produced by them. It (Ishvara) is the guru of even the earlier created beings, as it is not bound by time. Its appellation is pranava or the word AUM. Its (AUM's) repetition and reflection on its significance destroy all obstacles and bring consciousness of the omnipresent."

Thus, we see that the Eternal Energy is signified by AUM. Its repetition with a conscious mind about its significance leads to liberation from sensuous obstacles which come in the way of getting the mind thought-free for the purpose of meditation.

Naturally formed Shiva linga of ice inside the Amarnath cave (Kashmir)

Part IV
Evoking the Eternal Energy (Physical)

1. **Here are the seven different ways to evoke the Eternal Energy with mantra AU……..M….**

This Part is about the practical aspects of evoking the Eternal Energy through mantra AUM. This is the opening sutra that declares that the following seven sutras are about seven different ways of evoking the Eternal Energy.

The reader is once again reminded that this Eternal Energy is present in all of us but it has to be evoked. Time and effort to awaken this energy are variable in different human beings due to the results of their previous karma. The sum total of the remains of previous karma are present in the form of samskara. Because of different samskara, all of us are different from each other at birth and in our childhood activities, interests and aptitudes.

Some of us have to make more efforts to evoke the Eternal Energy and some have to make lesser efforts. It means that we have to pierce through the layers of clouds which cover this sunshine. Some have thicker covering than the others.

The programme given in the following seven sutras is worked out in such a way that you occupy your mind with AUM alongside your daily activities. You are concentrating on your deeds and keeping the mind void of any other thoughts which have nothing to do with your deed at that particular moment. You can do this practice and experience the results, rather than theoretically understand the concept used here.

2. **Take seven deep AUM breaths with slow rhythm while facing the east upon getting up in the morning.**

Upon getting up in the morning, turn towards east and take seven breaths while pronouncing AUM as has been described in Part I. You may not sing the mantra loud, but direct the breath properly so that the last part resounds in your head region. Your effort should be directed to making the breath deeper and its release smoother and gradual.

Evoking the Eternal Energy (Physical)

3. You are the AUM, you are inhaling the AUM, and the inhaled AUM is merged with the AUM within.

You are the breathing entity in this whole action. The sutra explains about your oneness with the cosmic energy during your normal breathing. Your entire being is AUM. The prana energy you are inhaling is also AUM, as the whole cosmos is the result of the combination of the Eternal Energy and the Cosmic Substance. This energy that you breathe inside you merges with the AUM energy within you. Thus, ultimately, the AUM is outside and the AUM is inside and the AUM from outside goes inside and merges with the AUM within you.

4. Do always the AUM walking.

During the day we walk a lot inside the house or outside the house. I suggest that you count how many steps do you take in a day beginning from when you get up from your bed and walk towards your bathroom until the night when you walk to your bed for the night's rest. If you find it impossible, do the counting for an hour everyday. When you do this exercise of counting the steps, you get consciousness of the activity and movement of the process of walking. If you find hard to count or you are forgetful, use a pen and a paper to write down. If you are lost half way in counting your steps, do not get discouraged and do the counting the next day. With repeated effort, not only you will be able to count your steps taken during one day, you will get aware about your bodily movements and your presence in space.

The counting of your steps should be gradually converted to AUM walking. Each time you take a step, pronounce AUM silently or loudly as the circumstances allow you. By doing so, your walking will not remain a simple and dull process of moving yourself from one place to another, but a movement of dance with the cosmic orchestra.

Technical details

When you pronounce with each step the mantra AUM, your mind is freed from all the other thoughts. The thinking principle of mind is called chitta. The nature of chitta (chitta vriti) is to have a thought process in chain, one after the other. There is never a stop and one thought leads to another with some direct or indirect link with the previous thought. Like this, the process goes on. By breathing AUM or walking AUM, we break the chain of thoughts and bring our mind to stillness. It has been already stated previously that when we attain the stillness of mind, the mind acquires the nature of soul and is connected to the Eternal Energy. The mind acquires a sattvic state gradually. Sattvic state of mind is the state of void, away from the sensuous and closer to the spiritual or the Eternal Energy of the soul. This is the yogic state of mind. Patanjali has defined yoga as "Yogaschitta vriti nirodhah" (Yoga is to hinder the nature of the thinking process).

5. Water that cleans, purifies and enlivens you is AUM.

While you are cleaning yourself by taking a shower or a bath, think of the living element in water. That is also AUM that falls on you and cleans you. The element water of the five elements is a purifier. Let it clean your body, purify your mind and give you impetus. Pronounce repeatedly AUM... AUM... AUM... and wish for the purification of your body and mind. Wish that all the irritants and troubles of your mind originating from rajas and tamas might be washed away with the flowing water.

6. AUM is the food and AUM is the taker of the food and AUM is pure health.

Before you take your food, prepare yourself for this by saying that the food you are going to consume is a part of the same Eternal Energy that you are made of. Both the visible and invisible entities are present in your food and you. Food is AUM and you, as a taker of this food, are also AUM. Once inside you, the food provides you the five elements that make three dosha and these are responsible for all the physical and mental functions of the body. Let this food provide you balance and harmony.

Rasa, five elements and balanced nutrition

For the readers who are not familiar with the Vedic concept of balanced nutrition, it is important to understand its concept with respect to the cosmic order. Our body is made of five elements, which make three dosha responsible for the mental and physical functions of the body, like the nervous system, digestive system, respiratory system, and so on. Therefore, we need a constant supply of the five elements to the body for the functioning of all our systems. Body is replenished with the five elements through breathing and nourishment. There are six major tastes in the cosmos and these are sweet, sour, saline, pungent, bitter and astringent. The total effect of each taste on the body is termed as rasa. Thus, the word rasa is not a translation of taste but it is the total effect of a particular rasa on the body. This is a pharmacological term in Ayurveda which is used to explain the effect of the products on the body in nutrition and pharmacology. Each rasa is constituted of two of the five fundamental elements. Thus, the substances we consume replenish our body with five elements. Each natural substance contains more than one rasa. Some exceptional natural substances contain maximum of five rasa. The substances with several rasa and also the rasa in great intensity are called rasayanas. Rasayanas are those substances which bring intense energy to the body and enhance immunity and vitality.*

7. AUM is the doer of your most difficult tasks and solver of your problems.

While working or during some other situations in life, all of us face some difficult moments. Many of us feel helpless at times or what we call stressed in various life situation. Besides that, many of us suffer emotionally in one way or the other in various relationships. Some are unhappy because their companion does not come up to their expectations. There are others who have different expectations from their children. Most people feel completely worked out in diverse situations and many get also sick while facing difficult situations in life.

---

* For more details, see my books, *Ayurveda, A Way of Life* and *Ayurvedic Food Culture and Recipe.* The details about the books are given at the back pages of the book.

We give ourselves importance and think that we can control everything. If we change our attitude, subdue our ego and realise the eternal within us, which is beyond 'I', and let AUM be the doer, we can make life easier for ourselves. It does not mean that you stop your efforts, but make your efforts by evoking AUM within yourself. Ego and lack of patience are two principal factors which make us suffer. Remember always that things happen when there is time for them to happen– not before and not after. Keep pronouncing AUM and keep making best of your efforts.

8. **The energy of AUM that flows through your body and through your fingers is the doer (and not you).**

There is an invisible Eternal Energy that makes the body of flesh and blood function. There is a subtle body within this body with its network of nadis or canals. The subtle Eternal Energy flows through them in the entire body. That Eternal Energy is the doer of all and not exclusively the physical self most of us identify with. If we understand this basic fact, keep our ego aside and accept AUM as the doer, we can get rid of suffering and stress.

AUM: The Eternal Energy

Part V
Evoking the Eternal Energy (Subtle)

1. For evoking Eternal Energy at the subtle level, concentration practices on every details of the body should be done.

As has been already explained in the previous parts of the book, there is a subtle body within the physical body. The process of evoking energy is done in various steps. Concentration practices should be done on diverse parts of the body to evoke subtle energy.

The energy of the subtle body is different from the energy you have due to your will power and determination. That is at the physical and rational level, whereas this energy we are dealing with is at a subtle level. Let me give you an example to make you comprehend this idea better. You have a piece of work to finish one particular evening but you are feeling tired. You have no choice and you take some coffee and begin to work. Later, you get very much involved in your work and forget about your fatigue. You have kept your deadline and went to bed very late. Next day you feel very tired due to lack of sleep the previous night. On the other hand, if you are able to finish your work with the invoked subtle energy, you will not feel tired the next day. However, to invoke the subtle energy, you need a long time practice and reach at a certain level of spirituality where your sukshma sharira (subtle body) can function. Following concentration practices with AUM mantra are suggested to evoke the subtle energy.

2. Concentrate on your ears to hear only AUM while you are chanting.

Sense of hearing is considered as the foremost sense out of all the five senses. The object of sense of hearing is sound and sound traverses through ether (space) which is the first of the five fundamental elements. Ether is the primary element, which makes it possible the existence of other four elements.

Evoking the Eternal Energy (Subtle)

A yogi's cave at Gangotri in the upper Himalayas

Chant AUM and bring all your concentration on your ears. Concentrate on the sound of your own chanting or you can use the AUM music CD as has been recommended earlier. Do this for at least five minutes every day for about 15 days. Try to do it at the same time every day. With repeated practice, you will obtain the mastery and will be able to invoke the energy in few breaths.

3. Visualise AUM in your eyes while chanting the mantra.

Chant the mantra AUM and visualise its figurative form in both your eyes. That means, each eye is converted into AUM figure while you are chanting the mantra. Do this also for five minutes every day for fifteen days.

4. Concentrate on a particular smell and chant AUM while getting lost in your olfactory sense.

Take something that smells intense and pleasant and is a natural product, like rose or jasmine or sandalwood oil or crushed cardamom or another similar product. Inhale from this product and chant AUM while concentrating on this intense smell. Do this exercise persistently every day, as has been described above.

5. Concentrate on your tongue while tasting something.

Evoking the Eternal Energy (Subtle)

Smear something characteristic on your tongue and chant AUM while concentrating on this taste. You can choose something which is pleasant for you and along with the concentration and chanting, visualise the AUM figure upon your tongue. Do repeated practice for at least fifteen days to attain the mastery.

6. Concentrate on your fingers while chanting mantra AUM.

This practice is to enhance energy in your fifth sense– the touch. Chant AUM and concentrate on your fingers. Visualise that the energy of AUM is flowing through your fingers.
Fingers are used for most of the work we do and also for healing practices like massage and other similar treatments. If the subtle energy flows well, there is a command at another level than brain to lead you to do right and hinders you to do wrong actions (karma) where the tactile sense is involved.

7. AUM is in your nabhi (navel).

According to the Yoga Guru Patanjali, the concentric energy point or chakra at the navel leads one to attain the knowledge about the labyrinth of the body. That means with this concentration practice, you develop intuition to know about the internal parts of your body and about your state of health. To evoke this energy, chant AUM mantra while concentrating on your navel point. Do the practice regularly in the beginning for five minutes every day. Then gradually make it a habit to send your breath several times a day to this energy point by pronouncing (silent or loud) AUM while exhaling.

8. AUM is in your Hridya.

Hridya or solar plexus, which is the region of heart, lungs and liver, is another concentric energy point. This is the location of the soul from where the subtle body emanates. Do the concentration practices in the similar manner as for the nabhi chakra. Mastery on this energy point gives you the knowledge about your mind and its three qualities. It helps balance rajas and tamas with sattva.

It is important to do first for several months the concentration practice on nabhi chakra and then begin on Hridya. It is a gradual journey to the profounder part of one's being.

Part VI
Benefits of the Eternal Energy

1. **AUM breathing provides you radiation, energy and beauty.**

It is observed that most people breathe very superficially and mechanically. The AUM breathing is the conscious breathing and it automatically imposes control on your breathing. It is aimed at prolonging your breath and thus ultimately provides you tremendous cosmic energy. With the result, you get a radiating complexion, more energy and attractive appearance. However, for attaining all this, you should do this practice several times a day. No special sessions or special time is needed for that. You can do the AUM breathing any time and anywhere. It is highly recommended to do AUM breathing in the morning upon getting up, before the meals, before beginning a new work and before going to bed at night. This gives rise to a relaxed state of mind for the important daily activities.

2. **AUM walking gives you the stability of the mind.**

Walking while pronouncing AUM mantra gives rise to strong and stable mental state and one develops the capability to make decisions with wisdom and ease. One develops self-confidence and self-assurance. One is not easily stirred with ups and downs of life and is able to remain unstirred even in difficult situations of life.

3. **Cleaning yourself while chanting mantra AUM purifies your mind.**

Keeping connection with AUM while you are taking a shower or a bath purifies your mind. It gives you sattvic energy and helps shed excessive rajas and tamas. A pure state of mind gives rise to harmony and balance in the thought process.

Benefits of the Eternal Energy

Gangotri

4. AUM chanting before eating gives you the equilibrium of the dosha and enhances your energy.

While reflecting on AUM, you get completely a still mental state and the food consumed with the peaceful mental state provides strength and harmony in the body and gives longevity.

> **5. AUM as the doer of your tasks takes away all stress and tension from you and makes you efficient.**

Stress is a mental state. It is a situation of being fearful of not being able to fulfil the expectations along with the feeling of helplessness. It is there because of our ego. Moment we let the higher energy take care of our tasks, the fear is gone and the work efficiency enhances. Some people may attain this with their faith in God or some deity or some pious holy place, and so on. But in the present context, by attributing the task to AUM, we are reaching the higher energy present within ourselves. Please recall the description given in the previous parts about the body being the temple of soul. Concentration practices with AUM help us to explore and utilise this internal source of Eternal Energy.

> **6. Evoking energy in fingers and concentrating on chakras with AUM**

provides you dexterity, healing capacity and creativity.

The fundamental theme here is the same as in the previous sutra– the realisation and utilisation of the Eternal Energy present within us. When we realise the presence of this energy flowing in the subtle body and flowing from fingers, automatically, we are able to use this energy. The creativity and healing are not from rational mind; they are from the higher realm of consciousness. Similarly, concentration with AUM on Nabhi and Hridya gives rise to skills of healing people at mental and physical level.

7. **Repetition of AUM by visualising your entire body provides you mental strength and courage.**

Chanting mantra AUM while visualising your whole body in its figurative form leads you to attain courage and strength. You can do this practice any time– while walking, while working or before taking a decision or before a special interview, and so on. This is an instant source of courage and strength in diverse life situations.

AUM: The Eternal Energy

Yogis at Gangotri

Part VII
Healing the Mind with AUM

1. **Repetition of the mantra AUM can help to get over mental afflictions.**

Mental afflictions are called klesha in yoga language. These are ego, attachment, aversion, longing and thirst for the sensuous enjoyment. All these give us pain and distress. Most of our day-to-day mental problems centre around afflictions. People are frustrated because they cannot fulfil their desires. Some want more money, the other want a particular man or woman, there are others who want children or still others whose children do not come up to their expectations. The fear of death or sickness or facing these two, jealousy, anger, aversion, hatred, etc. are several manifestations of afflictions.

Human beings wish for themselves the means of joy with material goods and sensuous love. When they have that joy and happiness, they want it in a steady state. This is contrary to the nature of the cosmos, as there is a constant change taking place and nothing remains forever. On the departure of these joys, they become unhappy and suffer. That is why, it is said that a wise person should partake in life as it comes.

In Sanatana dharma, a great importance is given to the control of mind and on developing mental capabilities. Repetition of AUM is instrumental in diverting one's mind from klesha and bringing it to the realisation of the Eternal Energy. We feel too involved with our physical, short-lived existence and that is why we suffer. Moment, we realise the entire cosmic reality as sanatana (without any end) and get connected to that sanatana element within ourselves; we can get rid of the afflictions and the pain.

In the following sutras, I have developed some simple techniques to get over afflictions.

2. Mental afflictions are the cause of pain and may also lead to disorders.

Mental afflictions not only disturb us mentally, but their repeated occurrence has an effect on our health. People end up getting mental or physical disorders or both, if they remain dissatisfied over a long period of time. Therefore, it is essential to get over an afflicted state of mind with a conscious effort.

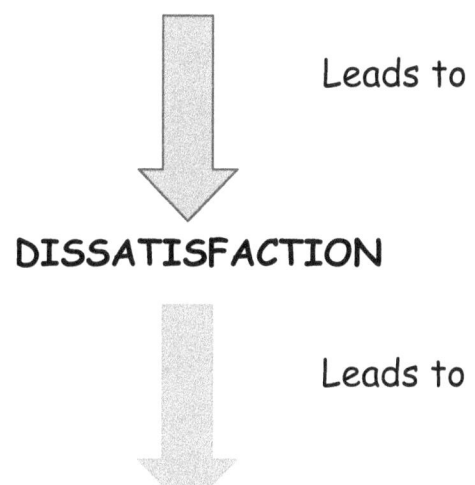

AFFLICTED STATE OF MIND

Leads to

DISSATISFACTION

Leads to

MENTAL AND PHYSICAL DISORDERS

3. Use dhaukani (bellows) AUM to control anger, aversion and hatred.

Until now, I have described the singing or repetition of mantra AUM in the classical manner. For healing the mind from afflictions, here are some techniques of AUM repetition with special pranayama exercises. This particular exercise is dhaukani pranayama along with the pronouncement of AUM.

With emotions of anger, aversion or hatred, one gets mentally disturbed. In fact these three emotional states are quite interrelated. The great sage of Ayurveda, Charaka has categorized these as 'suppressible urges', suggesting thereby that the human beings should suppress urge to anger, aversion and hatred with personal efforts, as they are harmful for health. The moment you feel that you are overcome by these emotions, get over these by doing dhaukani pranayama with AUM as described below. These exercises are meant to burn these emotions which cause mental afflictions. Dhaukani is an instrument which is used to blow air on the fire to enhance it. It is to push out the air with force and in a gush. The air is collected in a leather pouch and is blown out by pressing a handle attached to this leather pouch. In this breathing practice, you are going to copy dhaukani with your breathing. Following is the technique of rhyming AUM with Dhaukani pranayama.

AUM with Dhaukani pranayama

STEP 1

Learning the Dhaukani pranayama[*]

Sit still cross-legged or in a chair. Inhale small amount of air and simultaneously pull inwards your abdomen muscles as far as you can. Blow out the air with force and repeat this process rapidly. Do not move your shoulders or other parts of your body in this process. Repeat this for several days until you can do this effortlessly.

Caution: Do not do this practice until three hours after having eaten.

STEP 2

While you do the above-described practice, during the first part of retracting the abdomen and inhaling the air, you are doing the first part of AUM. You cannot sing AUM while doing this pranayama. It has an internal rhyme with your dhaukani practice. There is a little noise of air while you blow out the air. Render a tone of ....M to the rapidly gushing out breath.

---

[*] *Caution:* [*] *This practice should not be done by persons who have asthma or any other respiratory trouble or by those who are weak, feeble or anaemic.*

4. Recite Jara AUM to control attachment.

Jara means old age accompanied by degeneration and weakness. If you are over-powered by the emotion of excessive attachment towards worldly objects or persons, you need to realise the ever-changing nature of the cosmos to get rid of this klesha or affliction. Imagine yourself at the age of seventy or eighty. Think about the impermanence of all what exists. Neither you nor the objects and persons around you are going to escape the transformation caused by passing time.

In Ayurveda, there is a difference between Bridha avastha (being old and staying healthy and in harmony) and jara avastha (the old age accompanied by degeneration and weakness). Realisation of the last part of your life with singing of mantra AUM will make you become conscious of the futility of attachment. Therefore, I suggest that you invest your energy to be healthy and wise in future, rather than hankering after other persons or things.

Chanting of Jara AUM

Take few very deep breaths and enhance the capacity of your lungs to have slow and profound breathing. Begin to sing mantra AUM as described previously. During the first part with AU.... feel the energy within yourself. During the second part of nasal M let yourself completely lose and imagine yourself as old and weak. By the end of the singing M, feel yourself completely unable to move and exhale all the air. Revive yourself to youthful energy with the next inhaling and singing AU..... Repeat the mantra several times. You are undergoing the process of youth to old age by chanting one mantra. This process will purify you mentally and will help you to get rid of attachment with gradual practice.

5. Use mrityu AUM to control greed.

Mrityu means death. Human beings are overpowered with greed basically due to a false notion that they are going to live here forever. The basic fact of life is that all what we accumulate; we have to leave behind and depart empty handed from this world. Once we have the realisation of this, the affliction caused by greed will automatically vanish.

AUM: The Eternal Energy

I propose repeating of mantra AUM with a realisation of the end of life.

AUM in Shavasana

Shavasana is the dead body posture and one has to imitate a corpse. Lie down on your back and let yourself completely loose. Palms of the hands should be facing upwards. Feel the heaviness of your body on the ground. Start repeating very softly and slowly the first part of the mantra and imagine yourself sending this energy to your entire body. The energy circulates in your body and you exhale while chanting the second part of the mantra. After exhaling out all the air, feel your body without breath like a corpse. Imagine the end of your life for an instant. Resume the breath and the mantra again. Repeat this several times to have this intense experience.

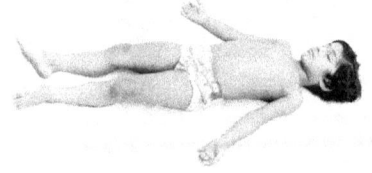

6. Use kapalabhati AUM to control kama.

Kapalabhati is a pranayama practice that involves inhaling towards the head region in a rapid manner.

When you are over-powered by sensuous desire that cannot be fulfilled and it becomes afflictive, do the following practice of kapalabhati pranayama along with AUM.

AUM with Kapalbhati

Sit down in a comfortable manner, preferably cross-legged. Start breathing in a manner as if you are pulling your breath upwards. Kapalbhati involves breathing rapidly and sending the prana energy to the head region. Coordinate this rapid breathing with AUM. Pull up the air with the tone of AU... and while exhaling, use the tone of ...m. It is not possible to make the sound of AUM, it is only a tone from the deeper part of the throat. Repeat this according to your capacity. In case you have problems, do it by giving some pauses of normal breathing in-between.

Caution: If you are unwell or suffer from any sickness or you are anaemic, do not do this practice. If you feel giddy, do not continue.

7. **Use AUM sadhana to stabilise and strengthen the mind.**

Sadhana literally means devoted labour for a particular aim. In the context of yoga, it is to do concentration practices in a regular, systematic and disciplined manner to achieve the aim of yoga. Aim in the present context is the repetition of the mantra AUM and to be involved with it all the time. At the primary stage, sadhana brings mental strength and stability. At an advanced stage, you achieve power for knowing the past and the future. Do simply the repetition of AUM with the aim of achieving the realisation of one's cause of being. Do the practice in the morning and evening in a regular manner. During the day, do the repetition by AUM walk and other practices told above.

Part VIII
Healing the Body with AUM

1. **Spiritual therapy is not independent of the rational and mental therapy.**

'Healing with AUM' implies spiritual therapy. In other words, it is the healing done by evoking the Eternal Energy. Therapies with other mantras, gems, music, pilgrimage, ashes from Yajna, all kinds of ceremonious healing, etc. will be under the category of spiritual therapy.

Charaka, the great sage of Ayurveda from 6th Century B.C. has described three kinds of therapies— rational, mental and spiritual. This sutra emphasizes that one should not apply exclusively the spiritual therapy, leaving aside the rational and the mental therapy. This can be very dangerous. Some people get fascinated by spiritual therapy and think that it is possible to be healed exclusively by one method or the other. However, in many cases, lack of rational approach and proper diagnosis is delayed and patient gets seriously sick.

2. **The three types or therapies should be applied simultaneously.**

Charaka has emphasized that the three kinds of therapies— rational, mental and spiritual should be applied simultaneously. Rational therapy includes proper diagnosis, intake of drugs, decoctions, diet, massage, exercises, oil baths, vapour baths, panchakarma or the five cleansing practices and so on. Mental therapy involves mental consolation by family, friends, guru or physician in order to enhance the mental strength of the patient so that he or she can mentally contribute to the process of healing. Yogic methods to stabilise the mind are also in the category of the mental therapy. Spiritual therapy is done either by evoking the Eternal Energy within or by faith in God or by certain rituals and ceremonies.

3. **Visible entity of the body is prone to degeneration whereas the invisible entity is eternal and beyond any change and destruction.**

Visible entity of the body is the physical self of an individual which is prone to degeneration. The invisible entity of the body is soul which is eternal. It is indestructible. It is this source we tap on for spiritual healing.

   4. **The Eternal Energy (invisible) that gives life to the material body (visible) can be used for healing.**

Body and soul are the substance and energy respectively and they form a being with the combination of each other. Neither of them can independently form a being. The Eternal Energy is the animating principle of the body made of five fundamental elements. By evoking this energy and directing it to the affected part, we can use it for healing.

   5. **Disorders come in the living body due to the blocked Eternal Energy.**

We have already talked about the subtle body and the flow of energy channels or nadis that take the subtle energy of the soul to each and every part. The body we perceive has an energy body or subtle body or invisible body (sukshma sharira) in it. This body emanates from the Eternal Energy of the soul and has its distribution system of energy to the entire body. Just like in the physical body, each and every part is reached with blood vessels, nerves, lymphatic vessels, and so on, similarly, the fine body also reaches to every part of the body to enliven it. If this energy is blocked and does not reach a particular part of the body or reaches it only partially, it speaks for an ailment due to some blockades.

6. **The essence of healing lies in removing the cover of darkness from the Eternal Energy and let it flow smoothly through the nadis (energy channels of the subtle body).**

The essence of spiritual healing in Vedic tradition lies in letting the Eternal Energy flow properly in each part of the body and getting rid of the blockades in the path of the flow of subtle energy. In other words, the two bodies– the physical and the subtle should be in complete harmony with each other and there should be a smooth flow of energy from the subtle to the physical.

Healing the Body with AUM

Through our five senses, mind remains busy with the world and gets completely involved with it. In day-to-day life, there is lot of action (rajas) and exhausted with the over activity of the mind, we fall into the phase of tamas. Tamas has also qualities like competition, jealousy, greed, etc. Rajas and tamas gradually distance the mind from the Eternal Energy by making a cover of darkness around the energy of the soul that hinders the light radiating from it. Sattva is the quality of stillness and peace. It is that quality which one attains by silencing one's mind. Silencing the mind means to have it temporarily detached from the world by ceasing the constant sensuous absorption from the outward activities. A thought-free mind stays in its own nature and is closer to the energy of soul than to the activities of the world. At this state, we get the flow of the Eternal Energy, which is used by the body to remove blockades and for healing disorders.

7. AUM is the medium to remove blockades from the path of subtle energy.

Repetition of the mantra AUM and concentration on its figurative form removes the cover of darkness which is build by rajas and tamas of the daily activities and takes us to the light of sattva. It helps silencing the mind and bringing the realisation of the Self, which is the soul. Our physical body is also a part of our 'self' but it is that which has temporary existence of a life span in that particular organisation and context. This means that we have a particular appearance, we are born to some parents in a particular space and we have certain surroundings of other human beings and environmental factors. All our surroundings get severed from our physical self at the time of death. The soul is the eternal and indestructible self of an individual with a particular karma coded on it and that decides for the circumstances of birth and situations in the next life. Although the body in the next life is also made of five elements, but their organisation is different due to the previous karma. The code of karma, which is saved on the soul and decides for the future, is in a way also the continuity of the physical self, as it is decisive for the appearance and qualities of an individual in next life. This is like genetic code in bigger space and time and samsakara is the long-term memory over a bigger span of time.

8. The affected area should be made as 'AUM zone' to revoke its sluggish energy.

The practice of the mantra AUM has been described in Part IV and V. If you do that regularly to bring harmony in your life, you will automatically get rid of your minor ailments. However, you will also have to follow the rational way of leading life that brings harmony according to the holistic Ayurvedic wisdom. The knowledge of pathya (holistic), apathya (non-holistic) way of life, as well as the knowledge of all that is hitkar (beneficial) and ahitkar (harmful) for the body is equally essential for learning to heal. The reason for this is that if you do the spiritual healing on one hand and do some antagonistic things to enhance the ailment on the other hand, it is not possible to achieve complete success in healing. Let me give you an example. You have a chronic cold and you begin your practice of AUM aimed at healing this minor but nagging ailment. However, you do not pay attention to the other observances, which are constantly enhancing this ailment. You get out of the bed uncovered in winter, you jump under the shower immediately after getting up, you drink cold milk and other cold beverages, and so on. That way you are enhancing your ailment and only spiritual therapy may not heal you completely. Therefore, simultaneously pay attention to the rational factors of healing.

For healing a specific ailment in a specific part of the body, concentrate on that part and direct the AUM breathing energy to that part. Do that as many times a day as you can and make this particular part of your body as 'AUM zone'. These are the yogic methods of healing and remember always that persistence is the fundamental for achieving success in yoga.

9. Breathing techniques along with the chanting of AUM should be focussed on the affected area.

Healing the Body with AUM

As you have learnt in the previous part of the book, the chanting of AUM or its silent repetition is associated with a specific kind of breathing. You have to coordinate the mantra, the breathing and the affected part to be healed. Take a deep breath and send that to the affected part. Gradually pronounce AU....M while your concentration remains on the affected part. This particular part gets into a higher realm of consciousness.

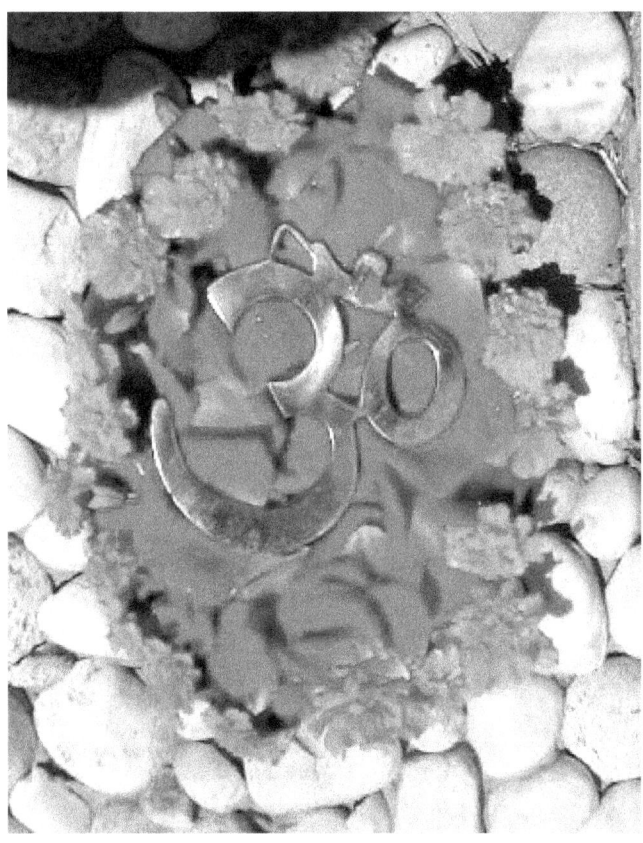

AUM: The Eternal Energy

It is important that you repeat the AUM mantra several times a day and it does not matter if you cannot do it for a long time at a stretch. You can do the practice while going here and there or taking a break of three minutes from work or while driving or waiting for a transport, and so on. Many people complain that they do not have time to do all this. All of us have lot of time when we are doing routine mechanical errands and our mind is occupied with absurdities. We need to make an effort to divert our mind to utilise that time for beneficial activities.

10. Concentration practices of AUM done while you are healthy can help you tremendously in healing at the time of need.

When you are sick and weak and need healing, you may not have so much mental energy and physical strength to do the healing. It is suggested that you do the practices described in this book regularly, so that you can apply them for healing at the time of need in a very spontaneous and natural manner. There is an old saying which states– you do not dig a well upon getting thirsty. In Chinese they say, you do not make weapons when there is already a war.

Process of healing is like a defence against the attack of a disorder. A regular practice of AUM mantra will help you in the time of need to defend yourself against ailments and disorders.

AUM: Your Protector and the Inner Guru

Nearly all languages of the world have adopted the word Guru from the tradition of Sanatana dharma. However, few understand its multidimensional sense. I experienced that many people in the United States had association with this word of an old bearded man who preached about some kind of religion or sect. Probably same is true for Europe or other countries of the world. Therefore, let me begin from the beginning to explain diverse meanings of this word so that you can comprehend better this concluding chapter.

Meaning and synonyms of the word 'guru'

First of all, let me give you the synonyms of the word guru in Microsoft word programme: spiritual leader, religious teacher. Maharishi, sage, spiritual guide, counsellor, leader, expert.

It is important to understand that the word 'guru' has nothing to do with the gender or beard or a sect. The word has diverse meanings and is used in different senses in Indian culture, tradition and sciences. Some of its fundamental meanings are heavy, weighty, great, large, extended, venerable, respectable, spiritual parent. Its antonym is *laghu,* which means small, light, tiny, etc. Guru means teacher in the traditional sense of the term and the word is also used for the present day teachers in the education system in our country. Traditionally, the education was imparted in the Gurukul, which literally means a clan of the guru. Gurukul is an ashram located outside the cities or villages. They have residential schools where education was passed on in all aspects of life in a holistic manner. Students do all their work themselves and these places are organised in such a way that the community work like cooking and cleaning is also done by the students. Even in the higher schools or specialised schools, other aspects of life are also taught besides specialisations. The traditional gurukuls still exist in a limited number. Here are some pictures from one of these Gurukuls in Uttarapradesh, about 70 Km northeast of New

Delhi. There are separate Gurukuls for boys and girls and this one is for boys.

In gurukuls, spiritual and lifestyle education according to the Vedas (including Ayurveda and yoga) is given equal importance, as mathematics, languages, physics, and so on.

Role of a spiritual Guru

There are also exclusively spiritual gurus. Spirituality is an ongoing process and in general people need initiation and feedback constantly to face the ups and downs of life. The importance given to spiritual education in India is noted from numerous TV channels exclusively for this purpose. Dearth for spiritual education and hunger for it in the masses in the West is realised when the Indian Gurus have huge following abroad. It is important to note that all gurus who are venerated by the masses are not necessarily the spiritual leaders in the real sense of the term. Some are business and money oriented and they enjoy comfortable lives. They exploit the masses rather than leading them spiritually.

Let us see what is the role of a spiritual guru. In the tradition of the Sanatana dharma, he or she is supposed to show you the way to realise the immense source of Eternal Energy you have within you. But you have to make a constant effort for 'discovering' yourself. An enlightened guru can show you this path with facility. However, it is not easy to find an enlightened guru. You need a strong desire, determination and perseverance to find the real guru.

According to the Sanatana tradition, a guru is not space and time bound. You may take the spiritual guidance from Swami Dayanand, Rama Krishana Parmahansa, Raman Maharishi, Anandamai Ma, who are great gurus from the recent past and can guide us still from their writings. My spiritual guru is Patanjali who lived 2600 years ago. Many people all over the world still find spiritual guidance through his book, *The Yoga Sutra.*

AUM: The Eternal Energy

AUM as protector

Throughout this book, I have talked about the inner subtle energy evoked by mantra AUM. There are techniques to develop the sattvic qualities like courage, self-confidence, fearlessness, and so on. Fear and anxiety over-power us and we lose our *vivek*, which is the higher realm of buddhi. *Vivek* is the enlightened state of mind and in this state, you cannot take any wrong decision or do any wrong action. By repeating mantra AUM regularly, you gradually get over the tamasic qualities, which is essential to achieve *vivek*. Even in the hardest of circumstances and during bad situations, your *vivek* protects you and leads you to act the best possible way.

I suggest that you use the symbol of AUM on all that is important for you and you want it to be protected. Everything is living and dynamic in this universe. Symbol and mantra AUM is a symbolic gesture to co-ordinate your Eternal Energy with that of the things and actions which are related to you. Put AUM on your home, car, computer or other tools of your profession. Similarly, repeat or touch AUM symbol before starting a new project, living in a new home, or driving a new car. Each time you start your engine of the car or switch on your computer, think of AUM. Repeat AUM and make the AUM movements with your cooking spoon while preparing meals. Begin your day with AUM looking towards the east where the sun comes and at the time of the sunset, do not forget few breathes of AUM by facing the west where it is disappearing, marking the end of that particular day. If you are a parent and tend to worry about your children when they are away, think of them and do the repetition of AUM to get away from your fearful mental state and to protect them. If you are stuck in some project, make AUM on everything related to that work and do the AUM japa to be more creative. Do the AUM walking and the AUM breathing. You will attain a still and peaceful state of mind and you will be creative and efficient.

Always remember that time is related to your state of mind. In a confused, fearful and worried state, the time slides away from you, and in a peaceful and still mental state, you have it in abundance.

Evoking the inner guru

A guru initiates the process in you to evoke your inner guru. Once you begin to experience the process of inner stillness and realisation of the cause of being, your Eternal Energy Itself becomes your guru. This light shows you the way. For achieving the inner stillness and the realisation of the Eternal Energy, you need to proceed with discipline and perseverance, and should have trust in the existence of this energy. Our day-to-day life is at the sensuous level. That means the common perception of reality is through our five senses. In the present context, we are talking about the subtle level, and that begins only when the sensuous ceases temporarily.

My suggestion is that through the simple techniques of this book, you help yourself to find your inner guru. Your efforts and perseverance will help you lead a spiritual life. That is where the real contentment and happiness lies.

Aum Shanti

AUM: The Eternal Energy

Kamakhya Temple in Gauhati, Assam representing the infinite feminine energy

About the Author

Along with a doctorate degree in reproduction biology in India, Dr. Verma studied Neurobiology in Paris University and obtained a second doctorate. She pursued advanced research at the National Institutes of Health, Bethesda (USA) and the Max-Planck Institute in Freiburg, Germany. At the peak of her career in medical research in a pharmaceutical company in Germany, she realised that the modern approach to health care is basically fragmented and non-holistic. Besides, we are directing all our efforts and resources to cure disease rather than maintaining health. In response, Dr. Verma founded The New Way Health Organisation (NOW) in 1986 to spread the message of holistic living, preventive methods for health care and to promote the use of mild medicine and various self-help therapeutic measures.

Dr. Verma grew up with a strong familial tradition of Ayurveda with a grandmother who had enormous Ayurvedic wisdom and was a gifted healer. She has studied Ayurveda in the traditional Guru-shishya style with Acharya Priya Vrat Sharma of the Benares Hindu University for 23 years.

Dr. Verma is an ardent researcher and is working hard to compile the living tradition of Ayurveda and spread it in the world through her books and other activities. She has published twenty three books on yoga, Ayurveda, Women and Companionship. The books are published in various languages of the world. Besides, she has published numerous scientific articles. Several other books are in preparation. She lectures extensively, teaches in Europe for several months a year, trains students at her two centres in India and gives radio and television programmes. A film on Ayurveda with her was made by German television in 1995 and was shown in 100 countries, in 130 languages. It was the first film on Ayurveda.

Dr. Verma has founded Charaka School of Ayurveda to train interested people with genuine Ayurvedic education so that they can further impart the knowledge of Ayurvedic way of life and save people from becoming a victim of charlatanry in Ayurveda. She is doing several research projects on medicinal plants and their combination in the form of remedies. She is the founder and chairperson of *The Ayurveda Health Organisation*, which is a charitable trust for distributing and promoting Ayurvedic remedies and yoga therapy in rural areas of India. She does regular lectures and workshops for school children in the rural and remote areas of the Himalayas to promote wisdom of traditional science and medicine. Dr. Verma gives seminars, lectures and teaches in the *Charaka School of Ayurveda* with guru-shishya tradition.

For more information and contacts for Dr. Verma's school and teaching programme see www.ayurvedavv.com and www.drvinodverma.com

Dr. Vinod Verma's Publications

1. *Patanjali's Yoga Sutra: A Scientific Exposition* (Published in English, Hindi and German).
2. *Ayurveda for Inner Harmony: Nutrition, Sexual Energy and Healing* (Published in English, German, Italian, French, Romanian and Hindi).
3. *Ayurveda a Way of Life* (Published in English, German, Italian, French, Spanish, Czech, Greek, Portuguese, Slovenian and Hindi).
4. *The Kamasutra for Women* (Published in English [America and India], German, French, Dutch, Romanian, Italian, Portuguese, Slovenian Hindi and Malayalam).
5. *Stress-free Work with Yoga and Ayurveda* (Published in German, English [America and India] and Hindi).
6. *Patanjali and Ayurvedic Yoga* (Published in English, German and Hindi).
7. *Programming Your Life with Ayurveda* (Published in German, French, English, Slovenian and Czech).
8. *Ayurvedic Food Culture and Recipes* (Published in English, German, Czech and Hindi).
9. *Yoga: A Natural Way of Being* (Published in English, German, French, Italian and Hindi).
10. *Companionship and Sexuality (Based on Ayurveda and the Hindu tradition)* (Published in English and German).
11. *Natural Glamour: The Ayurveda Beauty Book* (Published in German, Spanish and English)
12. *Losing and Maintaining Weight with Ayurveda and Yoga* (Published in English, Slovenian and German).
13. *The Timeless Wisdom of Ayurveda: A Scientific Exposition* (Published in English and German)

About the Author

14. *Prakriti and Pulse: The Two Mysteries of Ayurveda* (Published in German)
15. *Good Food for Dogs: Vegetarian nourishment based on Ayurvedic wisdom* (Published in German and English)
16. *Diet for Losing Weight* (published in German and English)
17. *Aum: The Infinite Energy* (Published in German and English)
18. *Pulse Diagnose in Chinese and Ayurvedic Medicine* (co-author for TCM Dr. Florian Ploberger) (published in German)
19. *Shiva's Secrets for Health and Longevity* (published in German and English)
20. *Healing Hands: The Ayurvedic Massage workbook* (in press)
21. *Prevention of Dementia* (published in German and English)
22. *Ayurveda for Dogs* (published in German)
23. Numerology: Based on the Vedic Tradition (published in English and Slovenian)

The Charaka School of Ayurveda and Patanjali Yogadarshana Society (Himalayan Centre)

The Charka School of Ayurveda (CSA) has been founded by Dr. Vinod Verma to spread the genuine classical tradition as well as the living tradition of Ayurveda in the world for promoting healthy living and preventing ailments. Its aim is to teach people a healthy lifestyle which enhances immunity and vitality and enables them to live a life with an optimum level of energy. For minor ailments, people should be capable of using home remedies, appropriate physical and mental exercises and nutrition.

CSA aims to bring genuine and practical aspects of Ayurveda to people and save them from Americanised and Europeanised distorted versions of Ayurveda and other forms of charlatanry that do more harm than good.

To achieve this purpose, CSA organises to train students in Europe who can further spread the message of Ayurvedic lifestyle and help people with genuine massages, purification practices, nutrition and other practical aspects of Ayurveda. The school is in association with the most learned persons of Ayurveda in India and several exclusive persons involved in health education in Europe.

The object of Patanjali Yogadarshana Society is to spread the message of Patanjali in the world. The wisdom of the Yoga Sutras is not only beneficial for the yogis but also for our day-to-day normal life. Its aim is to enhance *sattva* or the inner stillness and peace in the world as well as in the individual minds. With years of research on Yoga and Ayurveda, Dr. Verma has founded the Ayurvedic Yoga and has written a book on the subject.

Lectures, Seminars and Training Programmes

To get detailed information on the Charaka School of Ayurveda as well as our other programmes in India and Europe, visit our website or contact us by email.

The New Way Health Organisation .NOW.

A-130, Sector 26, Noida 201301, U.P., India

Tel. 0091 (0)120 2527820 or (0) 9873704205 or (0)9412224820
www.ayurvedavv.com www.drvinodverma.com
Contact at: ayurvedavv@yahoo.com

Himalayan Centre

AUM: The Eternal Energy

www.ingramcontent.com/pod-product-compliance
Lightning Source LLC
LaVergne TN
LVHW051601080426
835510LV00020B/3090